ONE WORLD UNDER PRAYER

For Morocco, North Korea and UK

CHARLES MWEWA

DEDICATION

For

Morocco, North Korea, and UK,

with love.

CONTENTS

DEDICATION · iii

CONTENTS · v

INTRODUCTION · vii

1 | PRAYER FOR MOROCCO · 1

Introduction · 1

Prayer Requests for Morocco · 4

Prayer for Morocco · 7

2 | PRAYER FOR NORTH KOREA · 11

Introduction · 11

Prayer Requests for North Korea · 20

Prayer for North Korea · 21

3 | PRAYER FOR UNITED KINGDOM · 25

Introduction · 25

Prayer Requests for UK · 29

Prayer for UK · 30

ABOUT THE AUTHOR · 33

SELECTED BOOKS BY THIS AUTHOR · 35

INDEX · 41

Christians are called upon to intercede for nations. It is alright to do so, and it glorifies God. In this series called *One World under Prayer*, the author pours out his heart for the nations of the world, without discrimination or prejudice. The administration of world affairs is at God's behest: "Let everyone be subject to the governing authorities, for there is no authority except that which God has established. The authorities that exist have been established by God."[1] He only appoints a select few to manage the world interests on His behalf.

National-interested Bible heroes prayed for their nations. Daniel confessed the sins of his nation.[2] The Psalmist, possibly King David, declared the strength and salvation of God for his nation.[3] Responding to King Solomon's prayer, God answered: "If my people, who are called by my name, will humble themselves and pray and seek my face and turn from their

---

[1] Romans 13:1
[2] 9:4-10; 17-19
[3] Psalm 46:1

wicked ways, then I will hear from heaven, and I will forgive their sin and will heal their land."[4]

Prayer for the entire world is necessary because it is God's.[5] We endeavor to return His gift of creation to Him by interceding for the whole world.[6] Prosperity and peace for the world rests primarily in prayer: "Also, seek the peace and prosperity of the city to which I have carried you into exile. Pray to the Lord for it, because if it prospers, you too will prosper."[7]

Indeed, God has dominion of all the world. In prayer, we remind Him to look kindly at His creatures and children and order their affairs.[8]

The governance of the entire earth is in God's hands, although He has entrusted it to mortal men.[9] And for nations to be great, they need God. Nations are not great because of the ingenuity of their people; they are great by the grace of God: "He makes nations great, and destroys them; he enlarges nations, and disperses them. He deprives the leaders of the

---

[4] 2 Chronicles 7:14

[5] Acts 17:26

[6] Psalm 33: 6-12

[7] Jeremiah 29:7

[8] Psalms 22:27-28

[9] Prov. 21:1

earth of their reason; he makes them wander in a trackless waste."[10]

God is the ultimate commander and adviser to nations. Nations that ignore Him do so ungratefully: "For lack of guidance a nation falls, but victory is won through many advisers."[11] Nations that ignore God's righteous fall, those that stand by His justice, rise: "Righteousness exalts a nation, but sin condemns any people."[12]

In the New Testament, Paul encourages prayer for nations, and He prays for them:

> For this reason, I kneel before the Father, from whom every family in heaven and on earth derives its name. I pray that out of his glorious riches he may strengthen you with power through his Spirit in your inner being, so that Christ may dwell in your hearts through faith. And I pray that you, being rooted and established in love, may have power, together with all the Lord's holy people, to grasp how wide and long and high and deep is the love of Christ, and to know this love that surpasses knowledge—that you may be filled to the measure of all the fullness of God. Now to him who can do immeasurably more than all we ask or imagine, according to his power that is at

---

[10] Job 12:23-24
[11] Proverbs 11:14
[12] Proverbs 14:34

work within us, to him be glory in the church
and in Christ Jesus throughout all
generations, for ever and ever! Amen.[13]

Accordingly, all people of the world need prayer for collective world success and tranquility: "I urge, then, first, that petitions, prayers, intercession, and thanksgiving be made for all people— for kings and all those in authority, that we may live peaceful and quiet lives in all godliness and holiness. This is good, and pleases God our Savior, who wants all people to be saved and to come to a knowledge of the truth."[14]

The Bible has strictly urged us to fear God and honor world leaders: "Show proper respect to everyone, love the family of believers, fear God, honor the emperor."[15] We do so through prayer, without slant or bias.

In this book, we pray for **Morocco, North Korea**, and **UK.**

c.m.

---

[13] Ephesians 3:14-21
[14] 1 Timothy 2:1-2
[15] 1 Peter 2:17

1 | PRAYER FOR MOROCCO

Introduction

Morocco is in North Africa. Its neighbors are the Atlantic Ocean and Mediterranean Sea. Morocco has been influenced by the Berber, Arabian and European cultures. The Marrakesh's medina is a mazelike medieval quarter and it offers entertainment in the Djemaa el-Fna square and *souks* (marketplaces). There ceramics, jewelry and metal lanterns are sold. Morocco's Capital City is Rabat, located in the Kasbah of the Udayas, a 12th Century royal fort overlooking the water. Morocco's currency is the Moroccan Dirham. And its official languages are Arabic, Standard Moroccan Berber. Morocco attained its independence on April 7th, 1956. It has a population of 37.08 million (2021) according to the World Bank. Morrocco has a parliamentary as well as the constitutional monarchy systems of government.

Moroccan Gross Domestic Product (GDP) stands at US$142.9 billion (2021). "Growth will recover to 3.5 percent in 2023 and 3.7

percent in 2024 as global economic tensions ease and foreign demand for goods and services rebounds. Since rainfall during the winter season has been higher than in the previous year, agriculture can contribute more strongly to economic activity."[16]

According to Wikipedia, "Christians in Morocco constitute less than 1 percent of the country's population Most of the Christian adherents are Catholic and Protestants. Christianity in Morocco appeared during the Roman times, when it was practiced by Christian Berbers in Roman Mauretania Tingitana, although it disappeared after the Islamic conquests. The Arabs started conquering the region of North Africa in the 7th Century and in 698 Carthage was taken. Indigenous Christianity in North Africa effectively continued after the Muslim conquest until the early 15th Century.

"During the French and Spanish protectorates, Morocco had significant populations of European Catholic settlers; on the eve of independence, an estimated 470,000 Catholics resided in Morocco. Since independence in 1956, the European Christian

---

[16] OECD, "Morocco Economic Snapshot: Economic Forecast Update (June 2023),"

population has decreased substantially, and many Christians left to France or Spain. Prior to independence, the European Catholic settlers had historic legacy and powerful presence. Independence prompted a mass exodus of the European Christian settlers; after series of events over 1959-1960 more than 75 percent of Christian settlers left the country.

"In 2022, the U.S. State Department estimated the current number of Moroccan Christians as more than 40,000. Pew-Templeton estimates the number of Moroccan Christians at 20,000. The number of the Moroccans who converted to Christianity (most of them secret worshippers) are estimated between 8,000–50,000. Since 1960, a growing number of Moroccan Muslims are converting to Christianity.

"Article 3 of the Moroccan constitution 'guarantees to all the free exercise of beliefs.' However, the Moroccan *Criminal/Penal Code* prohibits conversions to other religions than Islam. Conversions of Muslims to Christianity (either proselytization or apostasy) often occurred during the colonial period, when laws against such conversions did not exist.

"According to Article 220 of the Moroccan

Penal Code, 'anyone who employs incitements to shake the faith of a Muslim or to convert him to another religion' incurs a sentence of three to six months' imprisonment and a fine of 200 to 500 dirhams. Any attempt to induce a Muslim to convert is illegal. Foreign missionaries either limit their proselytizing to non-Muslims or attempt to conduct their work discreetly. In spite of these limitations, a 2015 study estimates some 3,000 believers in Christ from a Muslim background.

Prayer Requests for Morocco

In 2023, Morocco was ranked as one of the 30 countries in the world where it is most dangerous to be a Christian. In praying for Morocco, this backdrop is germane.

According to Wikipedia, Christianity in Morocco appeared during the Roman times, when it was practiced by Christian Berbers in Roman Mauretania Tingitana, although it disappeared after the Islamic conquests.

According to tradition, the martyrdom of St. Marcellus took place on July 28th, 298 at Tingis (Tangier). Since the Tetrarchy (Emperor Diocletian's reform of governmental structures in 296), Mauretania Tingitana became part of the Diocese of Hispaniae (a Latin plural) and hence in the Praetorian Prefecture of the Gauls (Mauretania Caesariensis was in the diocese of Africa, in the other pretorian prefecture within the western empire), and remained so until its conquest by the Vandals. Lucilius Constantius is recorded as governor (praeses) in the mid to late fourth century.

The painting of Augustine of Hippo arguing with a man before an audience with Charles-André van Loo's and 18th Century Augustine arguing with Donatists Christianity was introduced to the region in the 2nd Century AD, and gained converts in the towns and among slaves as well as among Berber farmers. By the end of the 4th Century, the Romanized areas had been Christianized, and inroads had been made among the Berber tribes, who sometimes converted *en masse.* Schismatic and heretical movements also developed, usually as forms of political protest. The area had a substantial Jewish population as well.

Donatism was a Christian sect leading to a schism in the church, in the region of the Church of Carthage, from the fourth to the sixth centuries. Donatists argued that Christian clergy must be faultless for their ministry to be effective and their prayers and sacraments to be valid. Donatism had its roots in the long-established Christian community of the Roman Africa province (present-day Tunisia, Morocco, the northeast of Algeria, and the western coast of Libya) in the persecutions of Christians under Diocletian. Named after the Berber Christian bishop Donatus Magnus, Donatism flourished during the fourth and fifth centuries.

"A powerful earthquake has devasted communities in western Morocco. The magnitude 6.8 quake struck on September 8, 2023, roughly 70 kilometers (40 miles) southwest of Marrakesh, at a depth of 26 kilometers (16 miles), shaking homes and causing thousands of deaths and widespread damage."[17] According to the Red Cross, "According to the Moroccan government, the disaster has claimed over 3,000 lives and left thousands injured. While aid is reaching more isolated regions, logistical hurdles [loom] due to obstructed roads persist."[18]

---

[17] NASA Earth Observatory, "Devastation in Morocco," September 11th, 2023

[18] British Red Cross, "Morocco earthquake: latest news and updates," September 22nd, 2022

Prayer for Morocco

Dear Father,

You are the God of all times, knowing the future from the past and the present. In fact, nothing happens without Your knowledge. Our Lord Jesus Christ warned, "And ye shall hear of wars and rumors of wars: see that ye be not troubled: for all these things must come to pass, but the end is not yet. For nation shall rise against nation, and kingdom against kingdom: and there shall be famines, and pestilences, and earthquakes, in divers places."[19]

Indeed, Lord, we are not troubled as You instructed us. However, we are concerned with those who have lost loved ones and friends. We are also concerned with those who might have perished unsaved. And our prayer goes to those who survived, but with disabilities and traumas.

Lord, we know of the challenges Christians face in Morocco. But we are still hopeful that You will not abandon Morocco. So, we pray,

---

[19] Matthew 24:6-7

heal Morocco of the trauma of the earthquake and use it to restore Morocco to a relationship with You. For the sake of the remnant that worships You in Morocco, protect Morocco from future earthquakes and give men and woman who love You a great opportunity to promulgate the Gospel of love and mercy and healing in Morocco.

Father, let the hope of Christ emerge into people's heart. Let them know that You love and care for them. Let Your prosperity and comfort also reign supreme in Morocco. May Jesus Christ be preached and accepted by the Moroccans, and may they find eternal life through Him.

Father, we pray against persecutions of believers in Jesus Christ in Morocco. Give them strength only You can, and like Paul, they shall not shun away from declaring the whole counsel of God, even in the face of prisons or death.

Lord God, our Father, we pray against the ravages of Covid-19 pandemic in Morocco. That You grant national wisdom to its leaders to provide relief and leadership to its population, including post-pandemic counseling and goodwill. May the economic recovery of Morocco be swift, and that life should abundantly revive the health of the nation. Protect Morocco from emerging diseases of the Covid-19-type.

In the name of Christ Jesus, the Merciful Healer, Amen.

2 | PRAYER FOR NORTH KOREA

Introduction

According to BBC news,[20] "For decades North Korea has been one of the world's most secretive societies. It is one of the few countries still under nominally communist rule. North Korea's nuclear ambitions have exacerbated its rigidly maintained isolation from the rest of the world. The country emerged in 1948 from the chaos following the end of World War Two. Its history is dominated by its Great Leader, Kim Il-sung, who shaped political affairs for almost half a century. Decades of this rigid state-controlled system have led to stagnation and a leadership dependent on a cult of personality. The totalitarian state also stands accused of systematic human rights abuses."

North Korea is located in East and Southeast Asia. The Capital of North Korea is Pyongyang. The country has a land area of

---

[20] North Korea country profile - https://www.bbc.com/news/world-asia-pacific-15256929 - accessed on September 22nd, 2023

about 120,540 sq km, with a population (2023) of 25.9 million people. The language spoken in North Korea is Korean. It is estimated that life expectancy in North Korea for men is 68 years, and for women is 75 years.

North Korea's dominant or supreme leader is Kim Jong-un.

According to the US CIA Factbook,[21] "The first recorded kingdom (Choson) on the Korean Peninsula dates from approximately 2300 B.C. Over the subsequent centuries, three main kingdoms - Kogoryo, Paekche, and Silla - were established on the Peninsula. By the 5th century A.D., Kogoryo emerged as the most powerful, with control over much of the Peninsula, as well as part of Manchuria (modern-day northeast China). However, Silla allied with the Chinese to create the first unified Korean state in the late 7th century (688). Following the collapse of Silla in the 9th Century, Korea was unified under the Koryo (Goryeo; 918-1392) and the Chosen (Joseon; 1392-1910) dynasties. Korea became the object of intense imperialistic rivalry between the Chinese (its traditional benefactor), Japanese, and Russian empires in

---

[21] https://www.cia.gov/the-world-factbook/countries/korea-north/ - accessed on September 22nd, 2023

the latter half of the 19th and early 20th centuries. Following the Sino-Japanese War (1894-95) and the Russo-Japanese War (1904-05), Korea was occupied by Imperial Japan. In 1910, Japan formally annexed the entire peninsula. After World War II, Korea was split along the 38th parallel with the northern half coming under Soviet-sponsored communist control.

In 1948, North Korea (formally known as the Democratic People's Republic of Korea or DPRK) was founded under President Kim Il Sung, who consolidated power and cemented autocratic one-party rule under the Korean Worker's Party (KWP). After the Korean War (1950-53), during which North Korea failed to conquer UN-backed South Korea (formally the Republic of Korea or ROK), North Korea demonized the US as the ultimate threat to its social system through state-funded propaganda and molded political, economic, and military policies around the core ideological objective of eventual unification of Korea under Pyongyang's control. North Korea also declared a central ideology of *juche* ('self-reliance') as an internal check against outside influence while continuing to rely heavily on China and the Soviet Union for economic support. Establishing a policy of hereditary succession in North Korea, Kim Il Sung's son, Kim Jong Il, was officially designated as his father's successor in 1980, assuming a growing political and managerial role until the elder Kim's death in 1994. Under Kim Jong Il's reign, North Korea continued developing nuclear weapons and ballistic missiles. Kim Jong Un was publicly unveiled as his father's successor in 2010. Following Kim Jong Il's death in 2011, Kim Jong Un quickly assumed power and has since occupied the regime's highest political and military posts.

After the end of Soviet aid in 1991, North Korea faced serious economic setbacks that exacerbated decades of economic mismanagement and resource misallocation. Since the mid-1990s, North Korea has faced chronic food shortages and economic stagnation. In recent years, the North's domestic agricultural production has improved, but still falls far short of producing sufficient food to provide for its entire population. Starting in 2002, North Korea began to tolerate semi-private markets but has made few other efforts to meet its goal of improving the overall standard of living. New economic development plans in the 2010s failed to meet government-mandated goals for key industrial sectors, food production, or overall economic performance. At the onset of the Covid-19 pandemic in early 2020, North Korea instituted a nationwide lockdown that has severely restricted its economy and international engagement. Since then, leader Kim Jong Un has repeatedly expressed concerns with the regime's economic failures and food problems, but in 2021 vowed to continue 'self-reliant' policies and has reinvigorated his pursuit of greater regime control of the economy. As of 2023, despite slowly renewing cross-border trade, North Korea remains one of the World's most isolated and one of Asia's poorest countries.

North Korea has a history of provocative regional military actions and posturing that are of major concern to the international community and have limited North Korea's international engagement, particularly economically. These include proliferation of military-related items; ballistic and cruise missile development and testing; WMD programs including tests of nuclear devices in 2006, 2009, 2013, 2016, and 2017; and large conventional armed forces. Following a period of heightened tensions between North Korea and the US in 2017, Kim in 2018 announced a pivot towards diplomacy, including a re-prioritization of economic development, a pause in missile testing beginning in late 2017, and a refrain from anti-US rhetoric starting in June 2018. However, despite high-level efforts to ease tensions during the 2018-19 timeframe, including summits with the leaders of China, South Korea, and the US, North Korea continued developing its WMD programs and, in recent years, issued statements condemning the US and vowing to further strengthen its military capabilities, including long range missiles and nuclear weapons."

"Officially, North Korea is an atheist state, although its constitution guarantees free exercise of religion, provided that religious practice does not introduce foreign forces, harm the state, or harm the existing social order. Based on estimates from the late 1990s and the 2000s, North Korea is mostly irreligious, with the main religions being Shamanism and Chondoism. There are small communities of Buddhists and Christians. Chondoism is represented in politics by the Party of the Young Friends of the Heavenly Way, and is regarded by the government as Korea's 'national religion' because of its identity as a minjung (popular) and 'revolutionary anti-imperialist' movement."[22]

"Christianity began to rapidly gain foothold since the late 18th Century, due to an intense missionary activity that was aided by the endorsement at first by the Silhak and Seohak intellectual parties, and then at the end of the following century by the king of Korea himself and the intellectual elite of the crumbling Joseon state, who were looking for a new social factor to invigorate the Korean nation. In the late 19th Century, the Joseon state was politically and culturally collapsing. The intelligentsia was looking for solutions to invigorate and transform the nation. It was in this critical period that they came into contact with Western Protestant missionaries who offered a solution to the plight of Koreans. Christian communities already existed in Joseon; however, it was only by the 1880s that the government allowed a large number of Western missionaries to enter the country. Protestant missionaries set up schools, hospitals and publishing agencies. The king of Korea and his family tacitly supported

---

[22] Religion in North Korea - https://en.wikipedia.org/wiki/Religion_in_North_Korea - accessed on September 22nd, 2023

Christianity. From the late nineteenth century, the northwest of Korea, and Pyongyang in particular, became a stronghold of Christianity. As a result, Pyongyang was called the 'Jerusalem of the East.'

"At the dawn of the 20th Century, almost the totality of the population of Korea believed in the indigenous shamanic religion and practiced Confucian rites and ancestral worship. Buddhism was nearly dead, reduced to a tiny and weak minority of monks, despite its long history and cultural influence, because of 500 years of suppression by the ruling Neo-Confucian Joseon kingdom, which also disregarded traditional cults.

"During the absorption of Korea into the Japanese Empire (1910–1945) the already formed link of Christianity with Korean nationalism was strengthened, as the Japanese tried to impose State Shinto and Christians refused to take part in Shinto rituals. At the same time, numerous religious movements that since the 19th Century had been trying to reform the Korean indigenous religion, notably Chondoism, flourished. Christianity became widespread especially in the north of the peninsula, as did Chondoism which aimed to counter Christian influence.

"North Korean revolutionary leader Kim Il Sung's writings address religion in the context of the national liberation struggle against Japan. Kim argued stated that if a religion 'prays for dealing out divine punishment to Japan and blessing the Korean nation' then it is a 'patriotic religion' and its believers are patriots and that in the context of a struggle for national salvation against Japan, religionists who share the agenda of liberation must be welcomed into the ranks. Kim criticized the protestant Christian creed, stating that while '[t]here is no law preventing religious believers from making the revolution,' the lack of action led to 'non-resistance' and psalms alone could not block the Japanese guns when 'decisive battles' were necessary."[23]

"According to a study by Ryu Dae Young, however: 'Contrary to the common western view, it appears that North Korean leaders exhibited toleration to Christians who were supportive of Kim Il-sung and his version of Socialism. Presbyterian minister Gang Ryang Uk served as vice president of the DPRK from 1972 until his death in 1982, and Kim Chang Jun, an ordained Methodist minister, became vice chairman of the Supreme People's

---

[23] Ibid.

Assembly. They were buried in the exalted Patriots' Cemetery, and many other church leaders received national honors and medals. It appears that the government allowed the house churches in recognition of the Christians' contribution to the building of the socialist nation.'"[24]

Prayer Requests for North Korea

Open Doors US advises, "Pray that the worldwide Church would wake up, see the North Korean church as our family and get on our knees to plead for strength, peace and ultimately, freedom, for our sisters and brothers."[25]

Thus, Open Doors US suggests to pray for God to protect secret churches in North Korea; for Jesus to be with the 50,000 to 70,000 Christian prisoners enslaved in North Korea's prisons for the Father to protect North Korea children; the Lord to keep the church prepared for when North Korea will be opened up; and for the Holy Spirit to mightily move over North Korea.

---

[24] Ibid.
[25] "5 Prayers to pray for North Korea now," www.opendoorsus.org

Prayer for North Korea

My dearest Father in heaven,

We present North Korea before, O Lord of Grace, that You will deal with North Korea according to truth, and not to what others have said or written about it. We know that through media, especially Western media, we may only see North Korea as a pariah, but it is only Your eyes which see truth.

So, we ignore all the talk and reports and bring North Korea to You, just as it is. Look kindly upon its citizens and leaders and action Your hand of grace upon it.

North Korea, Father, has not always been without Christianity. We pray, rekindle the flame of glory You once allowed to visit the nation, and cause Christian missionaries to have access to prisons, education and other public institutions, and there, bring and instill the power and goodness of our Lord Jesus Christ.

We pray for its leaders, especially, for the supreme leader, that You will give him wisdom and a softened heart, to seek what is eternally best for his people.

Protect him and his government, and give to them understand and freedom so that they may be good and judicious leaders to the people of North Korea.

We also pray, that they should come to know that Jesus Christ can protect them from dangers they fear, such as nuclear threats. May they come to a mutual understanding, not only with China, but with the rest of the nations of the world in forging a peaceful resolve for a peaceful world of tomorrow.

We endorse the prayer requests of the Open Doors US, and invoke Your blessings with answer to those prayers on behalf of North Korea.

Love, dear Father, love North Korea, we pray.

Lord God, our Father, we pray against the ravages of Covid-19 pandemic in North Korea. That You grant national wisdom to its leaders to provide relief and leadership to its population, including post-pandemic counseling and goodwill. May the economic recovery of North Korea be swift, and that life should abundantly revive the health of the nation. Protect North Korea from emerging diseases of the Covid-19-type.

In the name of Christ Jesus, the Graceful Lover, Amen.

3 | PRAYER FOR UNITED KINGDOM

Introduction

Wikipedia profiles the United Kingdom of Great Britain and Northern Ireland (United Kingdom or UK or Britain) as "an island country in Northwestern Europe, off the north-western coast of the continental mainland. It comprises England, Scotland, Wales, and Northern Ireland.

It includes the island of Great Britain, the north-eastern part of the island of Ireland, and most of the smaller islands within the British Isles.

Northern Ireland shares a land border with the Republic of Ireland; otherwise, the United Kingdom is surrounded by the Atlantic Ocean, the North Sea, the English Channel, the Celtic Sea and the Irish Sea.

The total area of the United Kingdom is 93,628 square miles (242,495 km2), with an estimated 2023 population of over 68 million people.

The United Kingdom has evolved from a series of annexations, unions and separations of constituent countries over several hundred years. The Treaty of Union between the Kingdom of England (which also included Wales) and the Kingdom of Scotland in 1707 resulted in their unification to become the Kingdom of Great Britain.

Its union in 1801 with the Kingdom of Ireland created the United Kingdom of Great Britain and Ireland.

Most of Ireland seceded from the UK in 1922, leaving the present United Kingdom of Great Britain and Northern Ireland, which formally adopted its name in 1927. The nearby Isle of Man, Guernsey and Jersey are not part of the UK, being Crown Dependencies, but the British government is responsible for their defence and international representation.

The UK became the first industrialized country and was the world's foremost power for the majority of the 19th and early 20th centuries, particularly during the 'Pax Britannica' between 1815 and 1914.

The British Empire, at its height in the 1920s, encompassed almost a quarter of the world's landmass and population, and was the largest empire in history; however, its involvement in the First World War and the Second World War, the cumulative crisis and the loss of prestige led to the decolonization of most of the British colonies and the eventual end of the Empire.

A part of the core Anglophonic world, British influence can be observed in the language, culture, legal and political systems of many of its former colonies. The UK's culture remains globally influential, particularly in literature, music and sport.

The United Kingdom is a constitutional monarchy and parliamentary democracy.

The capital and largest city of the United Kingdom (as well as the capital of England) is London, a megacity which, alongside New York City, is one of the world's two leading financial centers.

The cities of Edinburgh, Cardiff, and Belfast are respectively the national capitals of Scotland, Wales, and Northern Ireland.

Other major cities include Birmingham, Manchester, Glasgow, and Leeds.

The UK consists of three distinct legal jurisdictions: England and Wales, Scotland, and Northern Ireland. This is due to these areas retaining their existing legal systems even after joining the UK.

Since 1998, Scotland, Wales, and Northern Ireland also have their own devolved governments and legislatures, each with varying powers.

The UK has the world's sixth-largest economy by nominal gross domestic product (GDP), and the tenth-largest by purchasing power parity.

It is a recognized nuclear state and is ranked fourth globally in military expenditure.

The UK has been a permanent member of the UN Security Council since its first session in 1946. It is a member of the Commonwealth of Nations, the Council of Europe, the G7, the OECD, NATO, the Five Eyes, AUKUS and the CPTPP."[26]

Rishi Sunak is the current Prime Minister of UK.

Charles Philip Arthur George (Charles III) is the current King of UK.

The Pound Sterling (ISO code: GBP) is the currency of the UK.

---

[26] https://en.wikipedia.org/wiki/United_Kingdom - accessed on September 23rd, 2023

Prayer Requests for UK

In an article, the Guardian[27] reported that, "More people under 40 in England and Wales now declare 'no religion' than profess to be Christian – the first time the UK's dominant religion has been pushed into second place in any age group.

The striking census findings – which also show more than 50 percent of twentysomethings are not religious, compared with under 37 percent a decade earlier – are expected to fuel debate over whether state schools should still be required to provide 'broadly Christian' daily worship, and the role of the Church of England in parliament.

In the two previous decades when the Office for National Statistics (ONS) asked the voluntary question on religion, Christianity came out on top as a proportion of every single age group. But in an almost complete reversal of the picture seen a decade ago, there are now 9.8 million Christians aged under 40, but 13.6 million people with no religion.

---

[27] Robert Booth, *The Guardian*, "Census data suggests UK faces 'non-religious future', say campaigners," January 30th, 2023

Campaigners for non-religious people said the figures 'make plain that the UK faces a non-religious future' and called on the government to adjust public policy and 'renegotiate the place of religion or belief in today's society.'

Last week's rejection by the Church of England of demands to allow clergy to conduct same-sex marriages is likely to further the trend, said Abby Day, a professor of race, faith and culture at Goldsmiths, University of London, who said the church continued to show itself as 'radically out of step.'

'Christianity is fading fast because of generational change,' she said. 'The baby boomers, the millennials and generation Z are all turning away from Christianity.'

Andrew Copson, the chief executive of Humanists UK, said on Monday: 'Today's results only serve to underline the archaic place that collective worship and faith-based discrimination have in our schools.'"

Prayer for UK

In this prayer, heavenly Father, we recognize that there are issues that may be bittersweet for the churched and the unchurched, respectively.

First, we pray for the historic church, the Church of England in UK. This, Your Body, has through years been a bringer of good news to hearts and souls in UK. We pray that You continue to resuscitate it with focus on the truth, who is Christ the beginning and end.

Second, we pray for the young generation and, indeed, older generations who no longer see relevance in Christianity, that You soft their hearts towards authentic Christ-centered religion.

And third, we pray for the nation's leaders, that they will strike a relevant balance between the rights of the minority in UK and the plight of historical Christianity. In that request, Father, we ask for courage to cease practices that in themselves do not promote love and understanding, acts that may be politically correct, but spiritually condemnatory.

Father, heal the wounds of the past and restore loyalty to the truth, even to the Bible.

Indeed, Father, we pray, may "no religion" in UK, in fact, be "more religion," as in that, more people who are tired of religion, will find Jesus Christ to be the real and true religion.

Send, we pray missionaries to the UK, even as UK supplied missionaries to the world at the end of the 19th Century and the beginning of the 20th Century.

Lord God, our Father, we pray against the ravages of Covid-19 pandemic in UK. That You grant national wisdom to its leaders to provide relief and leadership to its population, including post-pandemic counseling and goodwill. May the economic recovery of UK be swift, and that life should abundantly revive the health of the nation. Protect UK from emerging diseases of the Covid-19-type.

In Christ Jesus' name, whose Kingdom He is, Amen.

Best Selling Author, Charles Mwewa (LLB; BA Law; BA Ed; LLM), is a prolific researcher, poet, novelist, lawyer, law professor and Christian apologist and intercessor. Mwewa has written no less than 85 books and counting in every genre and has exhibited his works at prestigious expos like the Ottawa International Book Expo and is the winner of the Coppa Awards for his signature publication, *Zambia: Struggles of My People.*
Mwewa and his family live in the Canadian Capital City of Ottawa.

SELECTED BOOKS BY THIS AUTHOR

1. *ZAMBIA: Struggles of My People (First and Second Editions)*
2. *10 FINANCIAL & WEALTH ATTITUDES TO AVOID*
3. *10 STRATEGIES TO DEFEAT STRESS AND DEPRESSION: Creating an Internal Safeguard against Stress and Depression*
4. *100+ REASONS TO READ BOOKS*
5. *A CASE FOR AFRICA?S LIBERTY: The Synergistic Transformation of Africa and the West into First-World Partnerships*
6. *A PANDEMIC POETRY, COVID-19*
7. *ALLERGIC TO CORRUPTION: The Legacy of President Michael Sata of Zambia*
8. *BOOK ABOUT SOMETHING: On Ultimate Purpose*
9. *CAMPAIGN FOR AFRICA: A Provocative Crusade for the Economic and Humanitarian Decolonization of Africa*
10. *CHAMPIONS: Application of Common Sense and Biblical Motifs to Succeed in Both Worlds*
11. *CORONAVIRUS PRAYERS*
12. *HH IS THE RIGHT MAN FOR ZAMBIA: And Other Acclaimed Articles on Zambia and Africa*
13. *I BOW: 3500 Prayer Lines of Inspiration & Intercession from the Heart: Volume One*
14. *INTERUNIVERSALISM IN A NUTSHELL: For Iranian Refugee Claimants*
15. *LAW & GRACE: An Expository Study in the Rudiments of Sin and Truth*
16. *LAWS OF INFLUENCE: 7even Lessons in Transformational Leadership*

17. *LOVE IDEAS IN COVID PANDEMIC TIMES: For Couples & Lovers*
18. *P.A.S.S: Version 2: Answer Bank*
19. *P.A.S.S.: Acing the Ontario Paralegal-Licensing Examination, Version 2*
20. *POETRY: The Best of Charles Mwewa*
21. *QUOT-EBOS: Essential. Barbs. Opinions. Sayings*
22. *REASONING WITH GOD IN PRAYER: Poetic Verses for Peace & Unconfronted Controversies*
23. *RESURRECTION: (A Spy in Hell Novel)*
24. *I DREAM OF AFRICA: Poetry of Post-Independence Africa, the Case of Zambia*
25. *SERMONS: Application of Legal Principles and Procedures in the Life and Ministry of Christ*
26. *SONG OF AN ALIEN: Over 130 Poems of Love, Romance, Passion, Politics, and Life in its Complexity*
27. *TEMPORARY RESIDENCE APPLICATION*
28. *THE GRACE DEVOTIONAL: Fifty-two Happy Weeks with God*
29. *THE SYSTEM: How Society Defines & Confines Us: A Worksheet*
30. *FAIRER THAN GRACE: My Deepest for His Highest*
31. *WEALTH THINKING: And the Concept of Capisolism*
32. *PRAYER: All Prayer Makes All Things Possible*
33. *PRAYER: All Prayer Makes All Things Possible, Answers*
34. *PRISONER OF GRACE: An I Saw Jesus at Milton Vision*
35. *PRAYERS OF OUR CHILDREN*
36. *TEN BASIC LESSONS IN PRAYER*
37. *VALLEY OF ROSES: City Called Beautiful*
38. *THE PATCH THEOREM: A Philosophy of Death, Life and Time*
39. *50 RULES OF POLITICS: A Rule Guide on Politics*

40. *ALLERGIC TO CORRUPTION: The Legacy of President Michael Sata of Zambia*
41. *INTRODUCTION TO ZAMBIAN ENVIRONMENTAL LEGISLATIVE SCHEME*
42. *REFUGEE PROTECTION IN CANADA: For Iranian Christian Convert Claimants*
43. *LAW & POVERTY (unpublished manuscript)*
44. *CHRISTIAN CONTROVERSIES: Loving Homosexuals*
45. *THINKING GOVERNMENT: Principles & Predilections*
46. *WHY MARRIED COUPLES LIE TO EACH OTHER: A Treatise*
47. *LOVE & FRIENDSHIP TIPS FOR GEN Z*
48. *POVERTY DISCOURSE: Spiritual Imperative or Social Construct*
49. *SEX BEFORE WEDDING: The Tricky Trilemma*
50. *QUOTABLE QUOTES EXCELLENCE, VOL. 1: Knowledge & Secrets*
51. *QUOTABLE QUOTES EXCELLENCE, VOL. 2: Love & Relationships*
52. *QUOTABLE QUOTES EXCELLENCE, VOL. 3: Hope*
53. *QUOTABLE QUOTES EXCELLENCE, VOL. 4: Justice, Law & Morality*
54. *QUOTABLE QUOTES EXCELLENCE, VOL. 5: Dreams & Vision*
55. *QUOTABLE QUOTES EXCELLENCE, VOL. 6: Character & Perseverance*
56. *QUOTABLE QUOTES EXCELLENCE, VOL. 7: Actions*
57. *QUOTABLE QUOTES EXCELLENCE, 1 of 20: Knowledge & Secrets*
58. *QUOTABLE QUOTES EXCELLENCE, 2 of 20: Love & Relationships*

59. *QUOTABLE QUOTES EXCELLENCE, 3 of 20: Hope*

60. *QUOTABLE QUOTES EXCELLENCE, 4 of 20: Justice, Law & Morality*

61. *QUOTABLE QUOTES EXCELLENCE, 5 of 20: Vision & Dreams*

62. *THE SEVEN LAWS OF LOVE*

63. *THE BURDEN OF ZAMBIA*

64. *BEMBA DYNASTY I (1 of a Trilogy)*

65. *BEMBA DYNASTY II (2 of a Trilogy)*

66. *ETHICAL MENTORSHIP: Missing Link in Transformational Leadership*

67. *AFRICA MUST BE DEVELOPED: Agenda for the 22nd Century Domination*

68. *INNOVATION: The Art of Starting Something New*

69. *TOWARDS TRUE ACHIEVEMENT: The Mundane & the Authentic*

70. *ONE WORLD UNDER PRAYER: For Camerron, Ecuador, and France*

71. *ONE WORLD UNDER PRAYER: For New Zealand, Poland, and Uganda*

72. *ONE WORLD UNDER PRAYER: For Malta, USA, and Zambia*

73. *ONE WORLD UNDER PRAYER: For Germany*

74. *ONE WORLD UNDER PRAYER: For Haiti, Iraq, and Russia*

75. *ONE WORLD UNDER PRAYER: For Chad, UN, and Syria*

76. *ONE WORLD UNDER PRAYER: For Burundi, Canada, and Israel*

77. *ONE WORLD UNDER PRAYER: For China, Egypt, and Venezuela*

78. *ONE WORLD UNDER PRAYER: For Greece, Mali, and Ukraine*

79.   ONE WORLD UNDER PRAYER: *For Morocco, North Korea, and the UK*
80.   ONE WORLD UNDER PRAYER: *For Belgium, Brazil, and the Burkina Faso*
81.   ADIEU PERFECTIONS: *A Satire*
82.   OPTIMIZATION: *Turning Low Moments into High Comments*
83.   ACING THE IMPOSSIBLE: *Faith in the Other Dimension*
84.   END GAME LAW: *Financial Mindset in Quotables*
85.   THE RULE MODERATION THEOREM OF GOVERNANCE: *An Introduction*

INDEX

3

38th parallel. *See* North Korea

A

Abby Day, 29
Africa, 24, 25
Arabian and European
    cultures. *See* Morocco
Arabs, 2
Augustine of Hippo, 5
AUKUS, 27

B

Belfast, 26
Berber. *See* Morocco
Bible, vii, x, 30
Birmingham, 26
British Empire. *See* Great
    Britain
Buddhism, 18

C

Capisolism, 25
Cardiff, 26
Carthage, 2

Catholic and Protestants. *See*
    Morocco
Celtic Sea. *See* Britain
Charles III. *See* Charles Philip
    Arthur George
Charles Philip Arthur George,
    27
Charles-André van Loo, 5
Chondoism, 16
Choson. *See* North Korea
Christ Jesus, 9, 23, 31
Christian, 23
Christian creed, 19
Church of England, 29
colonies. *See* Great Britain
Commonwealth of Nations, 27
Confucian, 18
Council of Europe, 27
Covid-19 pandemic, 8, 22, 30
Covid-19-type, 31
CPTPP, 27
Crown Dependencies. *See*
    Great Britain

D

Democratic People's Republic
    of Korea or DPRK), 13
Diocese of Hispaniae. *See*
    Morocco
Dirham. *See* Morocco

Djemaa el-Fna. *See* Morocco
Donatists. *See* Morocco
Donatus Magnus. *See*
    Donatism

E

economic recovery, 31
economy, 15, 27
Edinburgh, 26
England. *See* Britain
England, Scotland, Wales, and
    Northern Ireland. *See*
    United Kingdom of Great
    Britain and Northern
    Ireland
English Channel. *See* Britain

F

Five Eyes, 27

G

G7, 27
Glasgow, 26
God, 25
godliness, x
Gospel, 8
Graceful Lover. *See* Christ
    Jesus
Great Leader, Kim Il-sung, 11
Guernsey and Jersey. *See*
    Great Britain

H

holiness. *See* godliness

I

Imperial Japan, 13
industrialized country. *See*
    Great Britain
intercede, vii
intercession. *See* petitions
Irish Sea. *See* Britain
Isle of Man. *See* Great Britain

J

Jewish, 5
Joseon. *See* North Korea
juche, 13
justice, ix

K

Kasbah of the Udayas. *See*
    Morocco
Kim Chang Jun, 19
Kim Jong-un. *See* North Korea
King David, vii
King of UK. *See* Charles III
King Solomon, vii
Kingdom He is. *See* Christ
    Jesus
Kogoryo, 12
Korean. *See* North Korea

Korean War, **13**
Korean Worker's Party, **13**

L

law, **23**
lawyer, **23**
Leeds, **26**
London. *See* England
Lucilius Constantius. *See*
    Vandals

M

Man of War. *See* Christ Jesus
Manchester, **26**
Marrakesh, **1, 6**
Merciful Healer. *See* Christ
    Jesus
missionaries, **4, 17, 21, 30**
Morocco, **1**
Muslim. *See* Morocco

N

NATO, **27**
North Korea, **11**

O

OECD, **27**
Open Doors US, **20**

P

Paekche, **12**
Party of the Young Friends of
    the Heavenly Way. *See*
    Chondoism
Patriots' Cemetery, **20**
Paul, **ix**
petitions, **x**
Pound Sterling, **27**
prayers. *See* petitions
President Kim Il Sung. *See*
    Democratic People's
    Republic of Korea or DPRK)
Prime Minister of UK. *See*
    Rishi Sunak
prisons, **8, 20, 21**
professor, **23**
Pyongyang. *See* North Korea

R

Rabat. *See* Morocco
religion, **30**
Rishi Sunak, **27**
Russo-Japanese War, **13**

S

self-reliance'. *See* juche
Silhak and Seohak, **17**
Silla, **12**
Socialism, **19**
State Shinto, **18**

Struggles of My People, **23**, **24**

Supreme People's Assembly, **20**

T

Tangier. *See* Tingis

Tetrarchy. *See* Morocco

thanksgiving. *See* petitions

the West, **24**

Tingis, **4**

Tingitana. *See* Morocco

U

UK. *See* Great Britain

UN Security Council, **27**

United Kingdom of Great
    Britain and Northern

Ireland, **24**

United Kingdom or UK or
    Britain. *See* United
    Kingdom of Great Britain
    and Northern Ireland

V

Vandals, **5**

W

WMD programs. *See* North
    Korea

Z

Zambia, **23**, **24**, **25**, **26**

9 781998 788552